The Warren Smith Ski Academy
Academy Handbook Lesson 1

written by
Warren Smith

The Warren Smith Ski Academy Handbook Lesson 1
First Edition 2004

Edited, designed & published by Qanuk Publishing & Design Ltd
45 Mysore Road London SW11 5RY

Content
Warren Smith

Editing & Design
Isobel Rostron
Michael Kayson

copyright © Snowsport Synergy Ltd 2004
photographs © Snowsport Synergy Ltd 2004
www.warrensmith-skiacademy.com

ISBN 0-9548513-0-7
Printed by Alden Press, Oxford

A catalogue record of this book is available from the British Library.

the
WARREN SMITH SKI ACADEMY
is sponsored by:

swiss.com

volkl.com

oakley.com

sidas.com

dainese.com

mammut.ch

scottusa.com

the
ACADEMY HANDBOOK
is produced in association with:

SAASTAL

ifyouski.com

VALAIS SUISSE

BERGBAHNEN

WARREN SMITH - PROFILE

Warren Smith is one of Britain's leading professional freeskiers and an Internationally Certified Performance Coach. He has spent many years teaching recreational skiers, developing ski instructors and coaching racers all over Europe. He is one of the most innovative instructors working in the Alps today and has earned a name for himself for getting results for his students.

Warren is a member of the International Ski Instructors Association, a member of the International Ski Coaching Federation, a UK Snowsports Coach & Tutor, a British Free-skiing Competitor, a producer and presenter of the highly acclaimed tuition video series 'The Ultimate Learning Experience' and a Presenter of cable TV's 'Ski Tips', and holds a Diploma in 'Sports Psychology'.

Warren Smith Profile
www.soulsports.co.uk/warrensmith

CONTENTS
Introduction

Contents

THE HANDBOOKS

The Warren Smith Ski Academy has been changing and developing skiers' technique for over a decade. It has earned a reputation for getting results for people who are at the intermediate, advanced and expert levels of skiing.

The Warren Smith Ski Academy Handbooks were compiled after hundreds of requests from people who bought the Warren Smith Ski Academy DVDs. The Handbooks follow the same format as the DVDs - using the same headings and explanatory images - and so are the perfect compliment to the DVDs, putting down in writing what you see on the screen. The Handbooks fit conveniently into your pocket and you can browse them while you are on a chairlift or in the office lift.

Handbook 1 accompanies the Lesson 1 DVD and sets out the Academy's technique solutions for Carving, Steeps, Moguls and Freeride. The Handbook is divided into four chapters, one chapter for each discipline. Each chapter is a mixture of Theory, Exercises and Images, again divided into four key elements for each discipline. At the beginning of each element you will find a column which has been left blank for your own notes and thoughts.

THEORY, EXERCISES & IMAGES

THE THEORY
You will find an explanation of the theory behind each technique.

THE EXERCISES
The Exercises explain where and how to apply the Theory to your own technique, with tips and examples to practise on the mountain.

THE IMAGES
Give you a visual understanding of where you might be going wrong and what you are trying to achieve.

These three things combined will help you develop your skill and build your confidence to ultimately give you a sound skiing technique.

CARVING

INTRODUCTION TO CARVING

The aim of carving is to travel in each direction while spending the majority of the time on the edges of your skis - the skis cut into and carve arcs in the snow. Constant adjustments to the body help to allow the skis to carve and not skid sideways - it is similar to the way in which an inline skater carves 's' shapes down a road.

In this chapter we focus on four key ways in which you can improve your carving technique - with tips, examples and exercises to help you feel the sensation of carving, increase leg lean and angles, control the amount of pressure and develop power steering of the legs to give you the perfect carved turn.

FEELING IT

IMPROVE TURN INITIATION

THIGH STEERING IS POWER STEERING

PROGRESSIVE & DYNAMIC LEG LEAN

A
FEELING IT

'Feeling It' is about being aware of what your body and skis are doing as you execute the carved turn.

QUALITY NOT QUANTITY

Carving is not about how many turns you make or how quickly you make the turn. What you are trying to do is get your skis to carve in an arc shape through the snow. Many skiers have heard about the concept of carving, have seen a picture of what carving looks like or watched a video and then have decided to have a go. Some skiers occasionally succeed in making half a carved turn, but what usually results is a turn that is similar to a carving turn but with the skis skidding rather than carving through most of the turn. However, the art of making a carved turn is definitely achievable for all skiers. The first thing to do is to work on feeling the sensation of carving through a turn or in an arc shape. Rather than trying to make linked turns (this comes later), break down the turn into parts and follow the exercise opposite.

**EXERCISE 1
QUALITY
NOT QUANTITY**

**THE AIM
To prevent the ski from skidding during the turn and to feel the sensation of the ski carving through a turn in an arc shape.**

WHERE

Start on a flattish terrain, ideally on a green or gentle blue piste. The more complete your carved turn becomes, the more your speed will increase. If you try this exercise on a red run, you will move across the snow too fast to feel the sensation of carving.

How

Start by making a ¼ turn to get the basic feel (**fig. 1**). Don't rush the turn, and practise it until you feel the sensation of a pure carve throughout the whole manoeuvre. Practise the turn in both directions.

fig. 1 - ¼ turn

As you start the turn, allow the side of your uphill hip to move progressively across the skis towards the slope (**fig. 2**). It only takes a little movement for the base of the ski to tilt away from the surface of the snow. This causes the edge of the uphill ski to dig more into

fig. 2 - uphill hip moves progressively across

the slope, which in turn means the skis carve more effectively. This movement should be smooth, so don't rush it.

fig. 3 - ¾ turn

Once you have mastered the ¼ turn, try to make a ½ turn. Again practise the turn until you feel the carving sensation with no sideways or outwards skid. Practise turning in both directions.

Once you have managed to make a pure carved ½ turn, try making a ¾ arc turn (**fig. 3**). Then a whole turn.

THE RESULT
By the end of this exercise you should be able to feel the basic sensation of your skis carving across the hill without skidding at all.

Track Check - Self Feedback

One way to check whether you are making a carved turn is to look behind you at the tracks your skis have left in the snow (**fig. 4**). Your tracks will show you whether you are making a pure carve or whether your skis are skidding slightly as you turn (**fig. 5**).

If you are skidding, you will be able to see from the tracks in which part of the turn the skid is occurring. Once you can see this you will be able to concentrate on improving the part of the turn through which your skis are still skidding.

Linking turns

If you have practised Exercise 1 and resolved any skidding issues, you should now know the sensation of a pure carve. Using the same concept outlined in the exercise, try linking a few turns together. Again try this at first on flattish terrain. Make sure that your manoeuvre is progressive, slowly allowing your hips to move across your feet.

fig. 4 - check your tracks

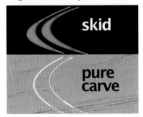

fig. 5 - skid vs. pure carve

CARVING

SKI TURNING CAPABILITIES

The reason a ski can turn so much across the hill with just a small movement onto the ski's edge is because of the shape and design of the modern ski. This is the built in 'Turning Capability' that all skis have (though some have more than others) (**fig. 6**).

fig. 7 - hourglass shape

fig. 6 - 'Turning Capability'

Most skis are shaped like an hourglass - wider at the tip and tail than they are at the waist (the middle of the ski's length) (**fig. 7**). Once you understand this built in turning capability, you can use it to improve your carving technique. You can then learn how much your skis can turn and how much you need to steer and tilt them onto their edge to be able to move across the hill as you want them to.

B

IMPROVE TURN INITIATION

POSITIVE CROSSOVER

One of the most important things to feel when you are carving is a 'Positive Crossover'. A Positive Crossover happens in the part of the turn when your body needs to move across the skis to tilt them onto the new edge.

This manoeuvre should start at the end of one turn, when the body starts to cross over the skis until they are tilted onto the new inside edges to start the new turn. This is known as the 'Initiation Phase' of the turn (**fig. 8**).

> **CARVING**
> **IMPROVE TURN INITIATION**
> - **POSITIVE CROSSOVER**
> - **KNOW YOUR HIPS**
> - **KNEE POSITIONING**

fig. 8 - the Initiation Phase, when the body crosses over the skis

Creating a Positive Crossover is the most intimidating aspect of any turn - no matter what level of skier you are. Some skiers lack the confidence required whilst others lack the skill. However, skilful and confident crossovers can be achieved by focussing on a couple of key areas of the body - your hips and knees. If these areas work properly without any blocks the movement will be smooth (**fig. 9**).

crossover

fig. 9 - a Positive Crossover without any blocks - hips and knees working smoothly

KNOW YOUR HIPS

Many skiers, even at the advanced levels, turn and crossover their skis without knowing how to make full use of their hips. Knowing when and where to move the hips can greatly improve the turn. Common problems skiers have include:

fig. 10 - shoulders are thrown across the skis

- throwing their shoulders across their skis first and following with a minimal hip movement (**fig. 10**).
- moving their hips too late in the turn, after they have already steered their feet to skid the skis through the Initiation Phase.
- moving their hips up and away from but not across the skis (**fig. 11**).

fig. 11 - hips are moving away but not across the skis

Work on some 'Hands On' exercises, to raise awareness of what your hips are doing and how to move them effectively whilst making a turn. Raising awareness of a part of the body is always a good idea before you start exercises.

On a gentle slope make a series of turns down the hill with your hands on your hips. Feel what is happening to your hips as you initiate a turn and go through the turning process.

After a few attempts you should understand better what your hips are doing and can move on to the 'Hips Encouragement' exercise overleaf.

CARVING

EXERCISE 2
HIPS
ENCOURAGEMENT

THE AIM
To encourage the hips to move across the skis in a positive way.

WHERE
On a shallow, quiet terrain, ideally a green or gentle blue piste.

How
Making sure to avoid other skiers, start to traverse across the slope at a slowish speed. As you approach the point at which you will start to turn, slowly put your hand on the side of the hip facing uphill and apply some pressure against it (**fig. 12, 13 & 14**).

fig. 12 - hand on hip, front view...

The application of pressure should be in the same direction that you want the hips to go during the turn - that is across the skis to help them cross over onto the new edges for the new turn.

Start with a very gentle turn shape, almost in the fall line (which is the straight line down the slope) of a flattish slope. When you feel

fig. 13 - side view...

comfortable with this manoeuvre, turn more and more across the fall line of the slope. With continual practice you will increase your understanding of what your hips will be doing.

THE RESULT
With continual practice you will build up a good level of skill and increase your understanding of when, where and how the hips should move across the skis to initiate a turn and overall make a better carved turn.

Once you have got to know your hips, you need to focus on where your knees are.

fig. 14 - and behind

KNEE POSITIONING

In an ideal world (**fig. 15**) all skiers would go from turn to turn with their hips, knees and feet the same distance apart, forming a symmetrical shape so their skis work at the same angle (**fig. 16**).

fig. 15 - an ideal world

fig. 16 - a symmetrical shape, with the inner leg parallel with the outer leg

In the real world many skiers don't form a symmetrical shape. Consequently when they turn they are not able to make a clean and smooth crossover because their knees are not the same distance apart as their feet. This blocks the Initiation Phase of the turn. Sometimes skiers have their knees too far apart. A more common problem is that the distance between the knees is less than the distance between the skis (**fig. 17**).

fig. 17 - knees inside the line of the skis

The part of the turning process that suffers most when the knees are closer together than the skis is the end of one turn and the beginning of another - right around the Initiation Phase.

The shape that the legs and knees form is known as an 'A-Frame' (**fig. 18**).

fig. 18 - the 'A-Frame'

Skiers form the A-Frame for a number of reasons. One is that as you learn to ski - from snowplough through to basic parallel - your knees spend most of their time inside the line of your skis. Because of this, as you begin to make parallel turns (either at ski school or self-taught), you learn to work the skis, how to steer the skis and what amount of pressure to put on them, and generally focus on what the downhill (or outside) leg is doing. Often this results in skiers developing a lazy inside leg or one that is just not as effective as the outer one (as it works and steers less efficiently). Because this inefficiency causes your inner leg to be slower, it leaves your knees in the A-Frame shape.

Another reason skiers turn with their knees and legs positioned in an A-Frame is because they do not create a strong enough edge platform towards the end of the turn from which to press against and gain support. This causes the outer ski to break away (it slips slightly downhill), forcing the downhill knee inwards, closer to the uphill knee and into the A-Frame.

More competent skiers (at the intermediate or even advanced levels) tend to be too aggressive and push through the end of the turn, forcing the outside foot sideways (**fig. 19**).

fig. 19 - too much outwards pressure

This actually causes the edge of the ski to break away from the surface of the snow leaving the knees closer together than the skis. The movement that brings the knees closer together can cause too much pressure against the edge of the ski for the ski to handle.

The first step is to accept that you are an A-Frame skier. Once you know this you can become more aware of what you are doing from your hips to your feet. Then you can become more conscious of your knees and the extra active role your inner leg must play as you steer and lean through your turns, as well as the extra sensitivity needed at the end of the turn to prevent the edge of your downhill ski from breaking away.

**EXERCISE 3
UNLOCKING
THE A-FRAME**

**THE AIM
To get the distance
between the knees the
same as the distance
between the feet.**

Where
On a gentle slope such as a green or
blue piste.

How
You need your hands for this exercise
so the first thing to do is to get rid of
your poles. Then as before break
down the turning process into single
turns.

As you initiate a turn, gently place your
hand on the inner leg. Using your
hand, pull your inner leg across (away
from the other leg) and into the turn
(**fig. 20 & 21**). Maintain a gentle
pressure on the inner leg throughout
the entire turn. Follow the same steps
turning in the other direction so that
the other leg is the inner leg.

Once you can complete the exercise
comfortably in both directions, return

**fig. 20 - hand on
inner leg**

**fig. 21 - hand pulling
inner leg**

to skiing normally (poles back again!) (**fig. 22**). Keep focussing on your inner leg and its change in position.

THE RESULT
An adjustment in your technique will make your inner leg more skilful, and will no longer block your turn initiation.

fig. 22 - and with your poles

EXERCISE 4
PREVENTING
BREAK AWAY

THE AIM
To prevent the ski from breaking away and the legs and knees from forming an A-Frame.

WHERE
On a gentle slope.

How
Think about what is happening at the end of the turn that is causing the ski to break away - it is usually effective to concentrate on keeping the right amount of pressure under the outside foot as you complete your turns. To achieve this, think about standing on the edges of your feet and turning the sideways pressure (**fig. 23**) into a downwards pressure. This forces the ski into the slope and increases the edge contact (**fig. 24**), giving you a stronger grip in the latter half of the turn.

fig. 23 - sideways pressure

fig. 24 - downwards pressure

THE RESULT
A stronger grip at the end of the turn, stopping the ski from breaking away and forming the A-Frame.

C
PROGRESSIVE & DYNAMIC LEG LEAN

CARVING
PROGRESSIVE & DYNAMIC LEG LEAN
- **TURN LIKE A RACER**
- **MORE SPEED TO LEAN WITH**
- **EARLY INNER LEG**
- **COUNTING A PROGRESSION**

TURN LIKE A RACER

Many skiers wish to be able to make the same type of dynamic turns that racers make (**fig. 25**).

fig. 25 - wishful thinking

To improve the dynamics of your own turns and to achieve the same sensations, you first need to understand how much you can lean your legs as you move through the turns. Then you need to understand how to make this leg lean a skilful and progressive one that steers the skis effectively and allows you to maintain balance and edge grip.

When it comes to leg lean, skiers tend to fall into one of two camps. Either they:

- are tentative or intimidated about increasing their leg lean and so do not lean enough; or
- lean enough but rush the movement through the first half of the turn and end up in a static position for the rest of the turn.

A progressive and dynamic leg lean on its own will not be enough. For the skis to work effectively and maintain good edge hold as you carve and make arc shapes in the snow, the carving movement must happen progressively. Each element of the turn - the leaning, the steering and the pressure control that you make with your legs - must happen simultaneously and must be skilful and precise. That is the only way you will cut a perfect arc.

The Exercises on the following pages should help you to do so - Exercises 5 (More Speed To Lean With) and 6 (Early Inner Leg) are for those skiers who find it difficult to allow themselves to increase their leg lean. Exercise 7 (Counting A Progression) is for those skiers who have the ability to lean well, but rush the movement during the first half of the turn.

When trying these exercises it is important to find an environment in which you feel comfortable so you can gradually let yourself feel the sensation of increasing your leg lean.

**EXERCISE 5
MORE SPEED TO LEAN
WITH**

THE AIM
To increase leg lean without fear.

WHERE
A flattish slope, ideally a green or gentle blue piste.

How
Break your skiing down into single turns. Make one turn and allow your speed to increase as you come out of it across the slope. If the slope is quite flat you can go fast without the worry of not being able to stop. When you are descending the slope with speed, progressively move your hips across your skis and allow your legs to lean into the slope (**fig. 26**). Keep experimenting with this movement until you feel that you have moved your hips further inside the turn, towards the hill.

fig. 26 - hips moving progressively

THE RESULT
Increased confidence in increasing your leg lean.

**EXERCISE 6
EARLY INNER LEG**

THE AIM
To become more skilful with your legs to increase the lean.

WHERE
A flattish slope, ideally a green or gentle blue piste.

How
As you begin to move and project your hips backwards as you start to make the arc of the turn, prepare the new inside leg to move by softening it early on in the turn (**fig. 27 & 28**). This will allow the hip to roll across early in the turn without any restrictions or blocks. This will help the leg to start to lean sooner. If the inside leg is allowed to continue to soften, flex and move across the skis through the turn, the degree of leaning will increase.

THE RESULT
With no restrictions this will leave you in a more dynamic and powerful position.

fig. 27 - soften...

fig. 28 - and some more

CARVING

**EXERCISE 7
COUNTING A
PROGRESSION**

THE AIM
To promote a progressive lean that is not rushed through the first half of the turn.

WHERE
A flattish slope, ideally a green or gentle blue piste.

How
Those skiers who rush through the first half of the turn will understand the benefit of counting progressively through the turn. Break the turn into four parts and count through from one to four in a slow, controlled manner (**fig. 29**).

fig. 29 - 1, 2, 3, 4...

THE RESULT
A progressive lean throughout the turn, from start to finish, and the maintainence of a constant pressure under your feet on the edges of the skis.

D

THIGH STEERING IS POWER STEERING

CARVING
THIGH STEERING IS POWER
STEERING

When you are carving or trying to carve through a turn, think about how you are actually physically turning your skis. It is very important for the steering motion through the turn to be positive and strong.

Most of the time, particularly when you are just learning to carve, a lot of attention is focussed on how the foot is being steered (**fig. 30**).

fig. 30 - foot steering

As the speed and dynamics of your turns increase, you should think about using the thighs rather than the feet as the main steering mechanism (**fig. 31**).

fig. 31 - thigh steering

fig. 32 - powerful steering action

This does not mean you should rule out foot steering completely, but generally the thigh is the core of the steering process whilst the feet fine tune the steering. There are exceptions to this rule and sometimes your feet might need to do a lot of the work.

Steering from the thigh gives a more powerful steering action throughout the whole turn (**fig. 32**). It will give the whole steering process a more solid and predictable feel and you will make fewer mistakes.

CARVING - A SUMMARY

Carving is about being able to make your skis carve an arc shape in the snow.

Your tracks will show you whether you are carving or skidding.

A ski has a built-in 'Turning Capability' which you can use to improve your carving technique.

Carving requires a 'Positive Crossover' of the body over the skis.

Understanding your hips and how to make full use of them will help to improve your carving technique.

Your knees need to form a symmetrical shape, not an A-Frame shape, for effective carving.

As well as needing a progressive and dynamic leg lean, each element of the turn (leaning, steering and pressure control) must happen simultaneously and be skilful and precise.

The thighs are the key steering mechanism for effective carving.

STEEPS

INTRODUCTION TO STEEPS

Steep slope skiing is something that fazes a lot of skiers and also gets the adrenaline rushing. To ski steeps, skiers have to adjust their stance depending upon the gradient of the terrain and the conditions of the snow.

In this chapter we focus on four key ways in which you can improve your steeps technique - giving you tips, examples and exercises to help you improve flex and leg extension, control pressure and develop powerful steering of the legs to give you power and confidence on the steeps.

CONFIDENCE
BUILDING

MORE LEVERAGE
MORE STEERING
POWER

STEEPER,
NARROWER

'CHECK'
THE SPEED

A
CONFIDENCE BUILDING

Having confidence in your ability to control your skis and have the right tecnhique is particularly relevant when you are skiing steep slopes.

STEEPS
CONFIDENCE BUILDING
- **NO DRAMATIC ENDINGS**
- **SKILFUL SKIDDING**
- **PUTTING IT INTO PRACTICE**

NO DRAMATIC ENDINGS

To build your confidence when skiing steep slopes, you need to think about what elements of the turn make your skiing more predictable and comfortable. For many skiers one of the most common problems on steep slopes is that speed increases suddenly and panic sets in. This often scares people away from the steeps, particularly if they have not had much experience skiing them. Even more experienced skiers, when trying to ski a more challenging or steeper slope, may find fear sets in on occasion, for example if they are not 100% sure about the outcome of the next turn and whether they are going to be able to control their speed as they rotate their skis.

SKILFUL SKIDDING

To create more control in the turn and to predict more what the outcome will be, you need to look at the angle you are setting the edges of the skis. When skiing on flatter terrain, the skis are normally tilted progressively onto a edge (**fig. 33**).

fig. 34 - too much edge angle for novice steeps

fig. 33 - typical edge angle on a flat slope

This supports you and provides a strong platform from which to push off from to get into the next turn.

Many skiers spend years learning and perfecting this movement. However, if the same movement is used when skiing on a steeper slope, unless you are well experienced and know exactly how to use the set of the edge, the stronger setting can be a bit erratic

and cause your skis to accelerate through the turn (**fig. 34**).

To prevent the turn from having such a dramatic ending, try to go from turn to turn with a continual pressure (**fig. 35**) under the foot rather than a turn that begins with soft pressure at the start and builds up towards the end.

fig. 35 - consistent pressure

EXERCISE 8
NO DRAMATIC
ENDINGS

THE AIM
To create a turn that has a more controlled ending.

WHERE
At first on a slope with a reasonable gradient. Then, after some practice, on a slope with a steeper gradient.

HOW
Make some turns, and as you do, monitor what you are doing by listening to the sound that your skis are making. If the sound builds up towards the end of the turn, you know that you are slamming the edges of the skis too hard into the slope (**fig. 36**). What you are trying to achieve is a consistent level of sound (**fig. 37**). When doing this you may notice that the skis remain at a flatter angle to the slope (**fig. 38**). This will result in a more predictable turn.

Once you have got used to practising this type of turn in a comfortable environment, go back to the steeper

fig. 36 - loud sound at the end of the turn

fig. 37 - a consistent sound through the turn

slope that was causing you problems initially. You should notice that the whole process is more relaxing and predictable than before (**fig. 39**). The edges of the skis do not always have to be set or tilted to the gradient that they are set to when skiing on more gentle terrain. The technique of being able to rotate the skis and control a skilful skid is very useful and something to be practised to help you become a better all round skier.

fig. 38 - skis at a flatter angle to the slopes

THE RESULT
An ability to be able to rotate the skis and control a skilful skid, bringing you more control when skiing on steep slopes.

fig. 39 - less edge angle, more predictable

B
MORE LEVERAGE, MORE STEERING POWER

STEEPS
MORE LEVERAGE, MORE STEERING POWER
- **WHY NO LEVERAGE?**
- **UN-CLIP TO FEEL**
- **THIGH HIGH & DRIVE**
- **IN PRACTICE**

Many skiers are unable to turn their skis effectively on a steep slope because they lack steering power. Normally this is because of flaws in their skiing technique, which show up in an area that may have been neglected when they were developing the ability to ski in parallel. Many skiers are unable to ski steep slopes with ease because they do not know how to flex all of their joints. An incorrect flexing of the joints leads to a lack of leverage to steer the skis. Most skiers think that they are flexing their joints correctly because they feel a nice up and down movement when they turn. The reality is that most skiers flex their knees and hips enough but they do not flex their ankles as much as they should (**fig. 40**) - if at all. You can get away with this when you are skiing on a reasonably gentle piste or on slopes that you feel comfortable skiing on, but it will cause you problems when you start to ski on slopes with a steeper gradient.

fig. 40 - no ankle flex, no leverage

fig. 41 - too stiff boots = no ankle flex

Skiers from beginner to basic instructor level may have this problem - and there are a number of reasons why, including:

- skiing in rigid boots that are too stiff for most skiers, not allowing them to flex their ankles sufficiently and get a sensitive enough feeling (**fig. 41**).
- a fear of the slope - skiing can be intimidating as a sport. The natural instinct is for skiers to drop their hips back making it impossible to flex the ankles (**fig. 42**).
- a misconception that arises from watching better skiers or from seeing a poster of a dynamic skier is the impression that a lower dynamic posture is good (**fig. 43**). Consequently skiers try

fig. 42 - fear = ankle flex blocked

to adopt a lower stance at an early stage. Rather than creating the lateral leaning of the legs achieved by the pro skier, lesser experienced skiers usually bend down lower - this results in them sticking their backside out, which is not always a pretty sight!

**fig. 43 - false leaning,
sitting back**

To overcome any of these
problems, the most important
aspect to work on is getting all of
the joints to flex together equally
and in relation to each other. Once
you understand this - perhaps the
most important thing for
succeeding - you can start to work
on exercises to improve your
technique and to develop good
flex throughout the ankles, knees
and hips together.

EXERCISE 9
UNCLIP TO FEEL

THE AIM
To feel more flexibility in the ankle joint than was there before.

WHERE
On a gentle gradient.

How
Un-do the clips around the middle or ankle area of your boots, on both boots (**fig. 44 & 45**). Then with the clips undone, make a few turns. Leave your bottom and top clips done up. Focus on whether you can feel more flex in the ankle joint than before.

fig. 44 - un-do the middle clips

THE RESULT
A better understanding of the amount of flex required in the ankle.

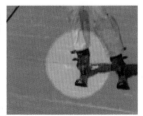

fig. 45 - clips undone

STEEPS

THIGH HIGH & DRIVE

It is also a good idea to look at the angle of the thigh. Usually skiers who have a lack of ankle flex in relation to the hip and knee flex usually have their thigh at an angle that puts their hips behind the balls of the feet. Ideally you want the hips to be on top of the balls of the feet, so think 'Thigh High'. This should make it even easier to feel the ankle flex (**fig. 46**).

fig. 47 - driving knees forward

fig. 46 - hips over the balls of the feet

It is also a good idea to focus on driving your knees forward (**fig. 47**). Try it standing still just flexing from your hips down through to the balls of your feet, with the knees driving forwards over the front binding.

Continued practice of these positions in a comfortable environment will help you find more flex in the ankle joint and have an equal flex through the three joints (ankle, knee and hip) combined.

IN PRACTICE

Once you have mastered this take your new found flex pattern and extra leverage onto the steeper slopes and check out the differences. If you've practised fully you should notice a massive difference and have much greater power at the Initiation Phase of the turn.

C
'CHECK' THE SPEED

Once your confidence has grown and your turns are more predictable on the steeper slopes, start to think about how you can make your steep slope skiing more dynamic. Now you have more control and more steering power, it's a good time to think about how to use the edges of your skis effectively.

RE-INTRODUCING THE EDGES

Skilful use of your edges on the steeps will allow you to control the desired direction of your skis more effectively. Your turns will also feel more lively and have a definite end to them. Once mastered, your confidence levels should shoot up even more (**fig. 48**).

fig. 48 - use of edges

**EXERCISE 10
EDGE CHECKING**

**THE AIM
Re-introduce edge
checking to your steep
slope skiing**

WHERE
A normal (fairly flat) gradient.

How
Start by making one turn. Towards the
end of the turn, steer both skis across
the hill and tilt them into the upper
side of the slope at a much greater
angle than you would normally. You
will notice that the skis make a loud,
short noise as you do this. To get the
edge angle you need (and the skis to
make this noise) you need to allow
your knees and hips to drop into the
hill (**fig. 49**).

fig. 49 - knees and hips
drop into the hill

The noise will become louder and
shorter in duration as you become
more skilful at tilting the edges of the
skis into the side of the hill to cause
the dynamic edge check - you will
also notice a more definite end to
the turn (**fig. 50**).

fig. 50 - skilful tilting

Practise the edge check movement on both sides, listening for a louder noise and a definite end to the turn (**fig. 51**).

THE RESULT
Creation of the edge angle that you need and a dynamic edge check.

fig. 51 - a definite end to the turn

DEALING WITH PRESSURE - SHOCKS

The more dynamically you dig the edges of the skis into the side of the slope to create an edge check, the more shock you will feel. To avoid being put out of balance by this, try to keep the muscles in the legs soft so that they are able to absorb the pressure that builds up. If you do not keep your muscles soft, you will notice that your waist gives. Another way to prevent the waist from breaking and cause the upper body to collapse forward, is to try to keep a strong core by retaining some tension in your torso (**fig. 52**).

**fig. 52 - strong core,
retained tension**

To achieve this your stomach muscles should not be totally tensed nor totally relaxed, but somewhere in between the two. On a scale of zero to ten, where zero is relaxed and ten is tensed, an ideal retained tension is about a five.

BACK TO THE STEEPS

When you feel comfortable that you can maintain a strong core, return to the steeper slopes. But don't jump in at the deep end - work up to your level of steepness progressively.

By now you should also be starting to become aware of where you are planting your pole, and how effective it is. If you can aim to plant your pole to initiate the new turn just as your skis have 'checked out' the end of the old turn, you will have greater confidence and greater stability to go into the new turn direction.

D
STEEPER,
NARROWER

STEEPS
Steeper, Narrower
- **Range of Steering**
- **Positive Extension & Pole-Plant**
- **Braquage for Narrow Steeps**
- **Short Swings, Dynamics**

As the slopes get steeper and narrower you will need to learn how to move your body more effectively and steer your skis to a greater degree to control your speed and stay in balance.

STEEPER

First we'll look at how to increase your range of steering - you need a greater range to slow your momentum and so keep your skis moving at a moderate speed. Ideally you should be able to steer your skis 180 degrees from the extreme of one turn to the extreme of the other (**fig. 53**).

fig. 53 - legs steer, hips don't

If you are able to do this you will have 100% control on the steep slopes.

Starting with the skis at right angles to the fall line of the slope, the true meaning of a good range of steering movement is the ability to steer the legs and skis a full 180 degrees from the starting position, across the fall line without any rotation of the hips (the finishing position of the skis is a right angle to the fall line). This is one of the hardest things to achieve. Most skiers can steer their skis through a certain angle (less than 180 degrees) without any problem, but if asked to steer to the extremes of 180 degrees, they usually rotate their hips. Unfortunately, rotating the hips - especially if you are skiing on the steep slopes - causes the whole of the upper body to rotate, which in turn flattens the skis. This normally results in the skis skidding and you falling over and "eating snow".

**EXERCISE 11
RANGE OF STEERING**

THE AIM
To increase the range of
the steering of your
skis.

WHERE
Start off on a flattish slope, before progressing to a steeper terrain as you feel more comfortable, ideally on hard packed snow.

How
Practise steering your legs across the hill and monitor the degree to which you can get your tips (without having to use your hips) (**fig. 54**). Progressively build up the range (using the leverage you learnt earlier in this chapter). Repeat continously.

fig. 54 - steer across the
hill, without any hip
rotation

THE RESULT
An ability to steer the legs through a repeated motion of 180 degrees across the hill. This will help you to attack a steeper slope with improved control, because the skis can always come to a definite halt when needed (fig. 55).

fig. 55 - a definite end to
the turn

POSITIVE EXTENSION & POLE-PLANT

To make your steep skiing more dynamic, you will need to develop a more positive extension up and forwards down the hill as you initiate the turn. Do it to a certain degree and you may find the skis even leave the ground slightly (**fig. 56**).

fig. 56 - up and away

Learning how to initiate the next turn positively and dynamically will benefit you both when the snow isn't perfect and also when you need a huge degree of energy to get the skis to turn. A strong pole plant will help you with to initiate the turn. As you make the turn plant the pole positively into the snow. At this point, project your hips and shoulders forwards and

down the hill. Make the projection by pushing up from the balls of your feet (**fig. 57**). As you do this, your skis will feel lighter, which will make it easier to manoeuvre them on the steeper terrain. How far you need to steer the skis depends upon the gradient of the terrain.

fig. 57 - push up from the balls of your feet

As you project more upwards eventually the skis will momentarily leave the snow. This will really help you when the going gets steep and the snow isn't perfectly groomed.

NARROWER

As the terrain gets steeper, it may also get narrower. It is a good idea to get used to skiing with less room to turn - you should first practise narrower turns without being in a demanding environment.

BRAQUAGE FOR NARROW STEEPS

To simulate narrow terrain, try to think about making your turns inside a narrow corridor. Imagine about 2 metres of width (the length of your skis, plus a little bit more) across the slope (**fig. 58**).

fig. 58 - imaginary corridor

Try to steer your skis within this distance. Typically skiers would jump into short radius turn, checking their edges - just because they know they can. But to keep within the principles we've used for steeps, if you jump into short radius turns of turns in steeper and narrower terrain (and so a new and difficult environment) your skis will accelerate and you will lose control. First, you need to work out how to stay in control and once you have done that, then you can focus on making the turns more dynamic.

First, try getting down your imaginary corridor with turns that don't have a great deal of edge. See if you can use the techniques you have learned to improve your steering power and range to pivot your skis slowly. This will prepare you to ski steeper, narrower terrain with more confidence and, more importantly, predictable speed control.

STEEPS

**EXERCISE 12
SHORT SWINGS,
DYNAMICS**

**THE AIM
To make the turn more
dynamic.**

WHERE
On a gentle gradient at first.

How
Focus on introducing the positive extension (described earlier) upwards, forwards and down the hill to release the pressure on the edges of the skis and to help you blast from one edge of the skis to the other (**fig. 59**). Initiate the turn using the pole plant. Steer the skis through the turn as you normally would and land them softly on the snow absorbing the shock with your legs, remembering to keep a strong middle body. As you feel more comfortable with these turns, try to feel or count a rhythm or tempo. Once you've achieved this, move to a steeper terrain.

**fig. 59 - a positive
extension**

THE RESULT
**A more comfortable feeling on
the steeps and narrows.**

STEEPS - A SUMMARY

Confidence plays a huge part in successful steep slope skiing. Ovecome fear by creating more control in the turn.

Monitor the effectivenss of your turns by listening to the sound the skis make at the end of a turn.

Steep slope skiing requires ankles, knees and hips to flex together to the required degree. Pushing up from the balls of your feet (with your hips over your feet) and driving the knees forward will help to achieve this.

Skilful use of edges gives you more control.

Muscles should be kept soft to absorb the build up of pressure. In addition a retained tension in the torso will stop your waist from breaking.

A good range of steering (a repeated motion of 180 degrees across the fall line of the slope of the skis is required).

A positive pole-plant at the Initiation Phase will make your steep slope skiing more dynamic.

MOGULS

1

INTRODUCTION TO MOGULS

Mogul skiing is another area that causes problems for recreational skiers. It requires skiers to develop a decent technique with much less leg lean and more leg steering than used when carving. In addition skiers need to adopt a closer stance and make pressure adjustments that are also quite different to those used when carving.

In this chapter we focus on four key ways in which you can improve your moguls technique - giving you tips, examples and exercises to help you improve the steering of the skis, absorption of the bumps, middle body strength, speed control and overall confidence.

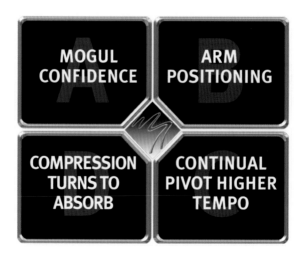

MOGUL CONFIDENCE

ARM POSITIONING

COMPRESSION TURNS TO ABSORB

CONTINUAL PIVOT HIGHER TEMPO

A
MOGUL CONFIDENCE

As with steep slope skiing, skiing moguls successfully depends on your levels of confidence. Making some changes to your technique can greatly improve this.

MOGULS
MOGUL CONFIDENCE
● **RE-CAP ON SKIDDING**
● **MORE SKID, MORE TIME**

RE-CAP ON SKIDDING

A common problem skiers have when skiing moguls is that they pick up too much speed, and lose control - this causes them to accelerate out of the bump (**fig. 60**).

fig. 60 - accelerating out

This happens mainly because skiers use a similar edging technique to the one that they use for skiing on piste. Most turns that you make on piste require you to tilt the skis onto their new edge quite early in the turn. If you do this when skiing moguls, you will find yourself speeding up and will never stay in enough control to experience a continuous run of moguls.

MORE SKID, MORE TIME

To control your speed, re-cap on the process used for skiing steeper slopes. Learn to rotate your skis without slamming the edge into the side of the hill. Also use a greater range of steering, which will give you more speed control - and make skiing the bumps more predictable (**fig. 61**).

fig. 61 - a greater range of steering

Using more skid in the turn will also help you to control your speed, and give you time to turn and pivot into the next mogul -

together this will also help you to build your confidence.

B
ARM POSITIONING

Another common problem skiers have when skiing moguls is where to position - and how to manage - their arms throughout the turns.

HAND DISTANCE

The wider the arms are apart, the harder it is to control the movement. Have your hands slightly closer together than you normally would when you are carving on piste. When you are carving with a good lateral movement a wider arm position helps you to balance when moving from side to side. There is less lateral movement when skiing moguls, so a narrow posture is more favourable (**fig. 62**).

fig. 62 - hand distance carving v. moguls

It also helps you to stop your arms and upper body from rotating. The further out your arms are when you are skiing moguls, the more prone they are to being pulled around with the momentum of the turns (**fig. 63**).

fig. 64 - elbows out,
outside of the hands

fig. 63 - arms too wide

fig. 65 - elbows out
= solid forearm

ELBOWS OUT

Sometimes even when skiers have learnt to adopt a narrower arm posture, they still find that their arms are pulled around a little bit, especially when their speed and performance level increases. When this happens, you need to think about keeping your elbows out of the line from your shoulder to your hand (**fig. 64**). Though this feels a much more static position, it is actually stronger and prevents your hands from being pulled out so much (**fig. 65**).

PRACTISE ARM POSITION

Practise making turns outside the moguls with your arms in this position. If you can get used to skiing in this way without having to think about other aspects of your technique you will learn the arm positioning more quickly. When you feel comfortable with it, introduce it into your bump skiing. Although this is typically a point of technique that is worked on at competition level, it is appropriate to think about at all levels - introduce this to your bumps skiing and you will feel an immediate difference (**fig. 66**).

**fig. 66 - practice makes
perfect**

C

CONTINUAL PIVOT FOR HIGHER TEMPO

Many skiers enjoy skiing a mogul field and can feel quite comfortable doing so. However, not many skiers can stick to or keep in a narrow line of moguls, especially those moguls that are tight and close together.

WHY PIVOT?

Most people, when faced with tighter, more difficult moguls, just traverse across the bumps or lose the line they are skiing because they lose control of their skis. To ski moguls succesfully you need to pivot over them. Skiers are usually unable to do so because they lack the ability to increase the tempo of their turns or the steering of their skis. One good way to improve your ability to steer faster and make higher tempo turns is to practise outside of the moguls. Eventually you will be able to make any kind of turn, even when the moguls get tight.

FINDING THE PIVOT OF THE TURN

Focus on finding your central point of pivot. This is usually located around the balls of your feet, but is only a true pivot point if your hips are over the balls of your feet (**fig. 67**).

fig. 68 - hip movement forwards...

fig. 67 - hips over the balls of the feet

fig. 69 - and backwards

When you ski on piste you normally make turns that require you to move your hips sideways across the skis (as explained in the chapter on carving). This crossover is what allows you to carve your skis. In the same instance you may find yourself projecting forwards (**fig. 68**) at the start of the turn and then backwards (**fig. 69**) as you ski through.

Your hips actually spend very little time directly on top of the balls of your feet.

**EXERCISE 13
RAPID STEERING**

**THE AIM
To increase the steering
speed to move the skis
quickly in the moguls**

WHERE
On piste at first and then progress to
moguls.

HOW
First (on piste) make turns with a short
to medium radius. Then progressively
build up the steering tempo.
Eventually you will reach a higher
tempo of steering while keeping a
constant pivot point (with the hips over
the balls of the feet (**fig. 70**) - this
makes your skis easier to manoeuvre.

**fig. 70 - hips over
the feet**

THE RESULT
**Back among the the moguls, you
will find what was impossible
before should now be achievable.**

D

COMPRESSION

TURNS TO ABSORB

If you watch skiers descending a mogul field, usually 20% of them are struggling, 60% of them are getting down without too much trouble and 20% of them you look at and think 'I wish I could do it like that'. The 20% that stand out do so because they are absorbing the moguls - by using 'Compression Turns' to ski over the bump.

DO YOU ABSORB?

With a Compression Turn you absorb the bump - in doing so the upper body remains upright and in balance and your legs flex up to the height of the bump (**fig. 71**). Then as you descend the bump, you start to uncoil the legs and extend them back out again, pushing them down, away from the body (**fig. 72**). This extension of the legs creates a friction, which controls your speed.

A Compression Turn is almost the complete opposite to the type of turn normally made on piste. On piste you

---

MOGULS
COMPRESSION TURNS TO ABSORB
- DO YOU ABSORB?
- BREAKING DOWN THE COMPRESSION
- LINKING COMPRESSION TURNS
- INCREASE RANGE OF MOVEMENT

fig. 71 - absorbing the bump

fig. 73 - on piste v. in the bumps

fig. 72 - extending legs into the trough

BREAKING DOWN THE COMPRESSION

Absorbing the bump is a pretty difficult thing to do and the success rate is not very high. There is already a lot to think about when you are skiing moguls, so it is tricky to introduce a new technical manoeuvre in addition to all the rest.

normally extend the legs to initiate the turn. In moguls, you flex the joints and pull your feet up underneath you as you initiate the turn, progressively pulling them up until the halfway point of the turn (**fig. 73**).

MOGULS

**EXERCISE 14
ABSORBING
THE BUMPS**

**THE AIM
To understand how to absorb
the bumps.**

WHERE

On easy terrain, such as a gentle piste.

How

Break down the turns bit by bit. Practise making a single Compression Turn (**fig. 74**). Flex the joints and pull your feet up underneath you as you initiate the turn. Continue to pull them up in a progressive movement until the halfway point of the turn. Then extend the legs back out again.

**fig. 74 - a single
Compression Turn**

A great way to help yourself feel the absorption of the bump when you are starting to learn how to make a Compression Turn is to use the natural terrain of the mountain. You can simply ski towards a bump on the slope and let your legs flex upwards to absorb the bump (**fig. 75**) - try to keep your upper body travelling at the same level (**fig. 76**). With enough practice on the

**fig. 75 - using the natural
terrain**

bumps, you should be able to develop a good enough range of movement to keep the upper body at the same level and let your legs soak up the whole height of the bump.

THE RESULT
A better understanding of how to absorb bumps in the terrain.

fig. 76 - using the natural terrain

LINKING COMPRESSION TURNS

Once you are comfortable with making a single Compression Turn, try linking them together while still on the piste. It is important to make sure that you are actually absorbing the bumps by tucking the heels of your feet up behind you (**fig. 77**) - the movement should not be made by your backside just sitting back.

fig. 77 - heels tucked behind you

It is essential that you get the movement right at this stage as when you move to the mogul field, you will need to be centrally balanced and able to make a succession of turns, without being pushed out of them by accelerating out of one bump to the next.

INCREASE RANGE OF MOVEMENT

Once you can feel you are maintaining your balance with your hips over the balls of your feet, you can progressively increase the range of your absorbing movement. Compression Turns are a great practice and skill development exercise, first to give you a better understanding of how to absorb the bumps and secondly to build skill and confidence before hitting the real moguls.

MOGULS - A SUMMARY

Successful mogul skiing depends greatly on your levels of confidence.

A different edging technique is used for mogul skiing than for on piste skiing.

Speed can be controlled by using a greater range of steering and more skid in the turn.

A narrower arm position, with the elbows out, should be adopted to prevent the arms and body from being pulled around by the momentum of the movement.

Successful mogul skiing requires you to pivot. Faster steering of the skis and an increase in tempo of the turns will improve your ability to do so. Your hips need to be over the balls of your feet to be a true pivot point.

Absorbing the bumps by using Compression Turns will help you ski moguls more successfully. The bumps should be absorbed by tucking the heels up behind you.

FREERIDE

1

INTRODUCTION TO FREERIDE

Freeride, powder and off-piste skiing is the ultimate buzz and the essence of the origin of skiing. This type of skiing is perhaps the most demanding and variable, and so requires adaptability for success.

In this chapter we focus on four key ways in which you can improve your freeride technique - giving you tips, examples and exercises to help you adjust to the changing terrains of freeskiing and become an all mountain freeskier.

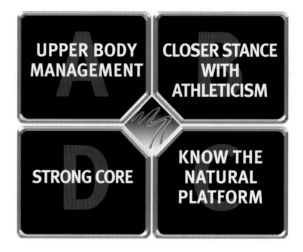

UPPER BODY MANAGEMENT

CLOSER STANCE WITH ATHLETICISM

STRONG CORE

KNOW THE NATURAL PLATFORM

A
UPPER BODY MANAGEMENT

If you have not had much experience skiing powder or freeskiing off-piste terrain, it is important to realise that certain techniques that work on piste do not work off-piste.

> **FREERIDE**
> **UPPER BODY MANAGEMENT**
> ● **SHOULDER AWARENESS**
> ● **SHOULDER MANAGEMENT**

SHOULDER AWARENESS

A common problem for many skiers when moving from on-piste to off-piste is how to manage their upper body, in particular their shoulders. When skiing on piste and making dynamic turns, skiers normally stand with rounded shoulders (**fig. 78**) - as this usually aids a more dynamic stance.

fig. 78 - rounded
shoulders

If you affect the same stance in powder or off-piste you may find that the position of your shoulders causes you to be off balance. When you are freeskiing you have to be able to absorb large pressure shocks caused by the ever-changing terrain. If your shoulders are in a forward position as you try to absorb the differences in the terrain no matter how much you use your legs to take the shock your shoulder position will cause your whole body to be hurled forward and to break at the waist (**fig. 79**) - this almost always results in you eating snow.

comfortable, move off-piste (**fig. 80 & 81**). This small change in the stance of your body will save you from having to put your skis back on in the powder just after that front flip that you didn't want to do.

fig. 80 - shoulders for off-piste

fig. 79 - break at the waist

fig. 81 - shoulders upright

SHOULDER MANAGEMENT

Concentrate on managing your shoulders for a while. Try this on piste first, then when you feel

B

CLOSER STANCE WITH ATHLETICISM

The distance you have your feet apart can also make a lot of difference to your technique.

WHICH STANCE SUITS WHAT?

At competition level, Giant Slalom skiers typically ski with a wide stance to maximise leg lean and edge grip. In comparison, a competition mogul skier skis with a closer stance in order to steer the skis rapidly and make tighter turns - leaning is not so much of a priority to them.

For freeskiing it is better to adopt a stance that is closer together than for piste skiing, similar to that used when skiing moguls (**fig. 82**). As your skis are sometimes submerged when you ski powder and off-piste terrain, if your feet are wider apart the skis are more likely to travel in slightly different directions. If your feet are closer together you will have a stronger foundation, giving you more consistency from turn to turn. Then your skis will generally spend more

fig. 82 - a good stance for free-skiing

fig. 83 - matching skis

lose the ability to make active and dynamic turns. Although their stance is more suitable for freeskiing, the reduced range of movement that results from clamping the feet together is bad. What you are trying to achieve is a close stance that retains the dynamics of your normal on-piste stance.

Practise a narrower stance on easy terrain, focussing on getting your feet closer together than normal. Make turns as you normally would - carving, short radius, steeps and turns with a large range of steering. Once you get used to skiing on piste with this narrower stance, you will be ready to tackle the off-piste terrain.

time matching each other on the crossover point of the turn and as you steer through the rest of the turn (**fig. 83**).

ATHLETIC NARROW STANCE

The narrower stance should also be an athletic stance. When skiers are told to put their feet slightly closer together, most just clamp them together and consequently

C

KNOW THE NATURAL PLATFORM

Not knowing how to steer the skis or deal with the build up of pressure against the edges of the skis to enable them to create a firm platform at the end of the turn is something else that catches a lot of skiers out in powder and other off-piste conditions.

WHAT IS THE PLATFORM?

When you make turns on piste, you are used to how the pressure builds up as you progress through the turn - the amount of pressure usually increases towards the end. With practise you are used to controlling the build up of pressure, to lean the legs and to steer the skis in the latter half of the turn to produce a strong platform from which to push off into the next turn and the new direction (**fig. 84**).

PLATFORMS IN POWDER

In powder and other conditions when the snow is soft and the skis are sometimes submerged, it does not take so much effort to make a good strong

fig. 84 - strong platform at the end of the turn

platform at the end of a turn. On-piste the platform is always created by the tilting of the ski and the edges of the skis biting into the snow (**fig. 85**).

fig. 85 - biting into the snow

Although you need the same elements off-piste or in powder, because the snow is softer or looser it builds up against the ski

and acts as a natural platform - kind of like a wall of snow being made against the ski (**fig. 86**).

fig. 86 - a build up of snow creates a wall of snow

This is what can catch people out. If you make the same effort to create the platform off-piste and in the powder as you do on-piste you can end up with too much of a platform because the added natural platform of snow. This will stop you in your tracks - something you may well have experienced if you have ever skied in deep snow.

BEING PROGRESSIVE

By becoming aware of this, you can start to work out how much you need to steer the skis and lean the legs to get the perfect supporting platform. It is worth focussing on not rushing the turn, but steering and leaning progressively (**fig. 87**).

fig. 87 - progressive steering

A rushed movement is more likely to create the type of platform that will stop you in your tracks - literally. Become aware of this when you are freeskiing and you will spend more time on your feet enjoying the ride (**fig. 88**).

fig. 88 - enjoy the ride

D
STRONG CORE

As you progress with your freeskiing and start to develop more speed and a more dynamic style it is important to focus on riding with 'Core Strength'. The faster you go the more amplified are the pressure shocks you get from the ever changing terrain. The waist is often the first thing to give when you are skiing. As with moguls a strong core, with no break at the waist, helps you to deal with these shocks.

FREERIDE
STRONG CORE
- **MORE SPEED, MORE SHOCK**
- **GETTING A STRONG MIDDLE BODY**

MORE SPEED, MORE SHOCK

As explained earlier, the core strength comes from your stomach muscles. The best way to identify these muscles is to simply pull your stomach in away from your waistband (**fig. 89**).

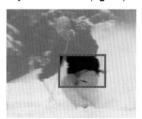

fig. 89 - core strength area

If you can train yourself to ski with a strong middle body strength you will be better supported and more ready to absorb the pressure. Skiing off-piste and putting in longer radius turns will really test you because unlike in moguls, you can't predict when you will need to adapt to a change in the terrain (**fig. 90**).

fig. 91 - 5 is the magic number

fig. 90 - unpredictable terrain!

GETTING A STRONG MIDDLE BODY

This middle body strength (or retained tension) is best quantified on the scale used earlier - again a 5 is the ideal score (**fig. 91**). This will keep you flexible enough to move and strong enough at the waist to prevent the upper body from collapsing forward.

FREERIDE - A SUMMARY

Management of the upper body, particularly the shoulders, is key to successful freeriding.

For freeriding you need to adopt a closer stance than the one you adopt for skiing on piste. This stance also need to be athletic.

A strong platform builds more easily in soft or deep snow. So you are not caught out by this you need to steer and lean the legs progressively.

As with steep slope skiing, the core strength required to overcome pressure shocks from the terrain comes from the stomach muscles.

Most importantly with freeskiing you must enjoy the ride.

A FINAL WORD

We hope you have learned something from the images, explanations and exercises in this book. Whether you are looking at performance carving, steep slopes, hitting the moguls or freeskiing in glorious powder, use the exercises to develop your skill level. Don't just try them once when you are away skiing, especially if you are having a bad day, also try them at your local dry ski slope or snow slope. Using these types of development drills in this way you can improve your skill level before you hit the mountains. Keep the ideas in your head, or make notes and keep the book on you when you go skiing so you can re-cap on the points and jog your memory. Combined practise will make you into a good all mountain skier.

Good luck with changing your skiing and hopefully catch up with you at the Academy in Verbier in the winter or Saas-Fee in the summer.

All the best
Warren Smith

INDEX

INDEX

APPENDIX OF EXERCISES

CARVING

STEEPS

MOGULS

let warren look after your skiing...

VBR

verbier

val de bagnes

"indispensable for skiers and
boarders alike"
Richard Cowper, Financial Times

by isobel rostron & michael kayson

the snowmole guide

and we'll look after the rest

planning your trip - in resort - on the slopes

pocket guidebooks

other titles in the range:

THE WARREN SMITH SKI ACADEMY HANDBOOK SERIES

The next two Handbooks in the series are also available to buy, from major outdoor retailers and major bookstores, and direct from the Warren Smith Ski Academy.

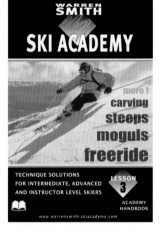

LESSON 2
£9.99

LESSON 3
£9.99

THE WARREN SMITH SKI ACADEMY DVD SERIES

The successful formula used by the Warren Smith Ski Academy to build confidence and skill development is available on DVD. Designed to help intermediates, advanced and expert skiers they are recommended by Ski & Board, the Daily Mail Ski & Snowboard, the London Ski Show, The Sunday Times, The Mail on Sunday, the Independent on Sunday, Capital Radio, ITV, Men's Health, Esquire and ifyouski.com

Priced at £16.99, the DVD is available from major outdoor retailers. The DVDs can be ordered on the Mail Order Hotline (+44 (0)1525 374757) or by email (sales@snowsportsynergy.com). Visa and MasterCard accepted. Mail Order guarantees delivery within 2 or 3 days.

LESSON 1 gives solutions for Carving, Steeps, Moguls and Freeskiing, with technical explanations, exercises and skill development for the 4 topics to help you become a confident all mountain skiers. There is also a special freeride safety explanation by top British guide Nick Parks, additional footage on 'Ski Biomechanics', 'Physiology', 'Ski Maintenance' and the actual script written by Warren for the programme.

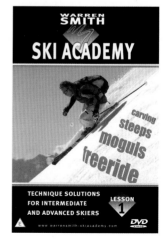

Lesson 2 continues on from where Lesson 1 left off. Once again split into Carving, Steeps, Moguls and Freeride, there are more exercises, tips, and explanations to help you to take your skiing to the next level. As with Lesson 1, the learning process is progressive and works under the philosophy of matching skill development with confidence building. DVD Extras include 'Skier Cross training', 'Ski Biomechanics continued', 'Safety Check', 'Pilates Core Strength Training Off Skis', 'Mountain Bike' and the script for the programme.

Lesson 3 gives intermediate, advanced and expert technique solutions for Carving, Steeps, Moguls and Freeskiing (powder/off-piste). It is also designed to aid 'GAP year ski instructor' level skiers. DVD extras include 'Dry Land Training', 'on Mountain Warm-Up', 'Skiercross Introduction' and 'More Mountain Bike'.

THE WARREN SMITH SKI ACADEMY

Based in Verbier, Switzerland, courses at the Warren Smith Ski Academy cater for intermediate, advance and expert skiers. The concept of the courses is to build an individual's skill and confidence to enable them to ski the whole mountain and not be restricted by terrain.

Courses and camps cover a wide range of the skiing spectrum - Personal Performance, Freeride/Powder, New School Freestyle, Heliskiing, Moguls, Race Training, Instructor Training, and Biomechanics - and you can choose which area to concentrate on if you wish. You can also be advised on what might be best for you.

GROUP COURSES last for 5 days (10am-3pm) and cover the main topics of Moguls, Powder, Steeps and Carving. Skills are developed during the course by practising specific exercises that benefit the main topics. The new levels of skill are progressively tested on suitable terrain to build confidence. As all skiers have different strengths and weaknesses each skier is looked at individually. Video Analysis is used 1-2 times during the course depending on weather conditions. An analysis of ski equipment is also part of the course, to educate skiers on how to get more out of their kit and understand it in greater depth.

PRIVATE COACHING is also available upon request, for a full day (10am-3pm) or a half day (10am-12:30pm or 1pm-3:30pm). The content of the private coaching is specific to what the client wants to do and what the client needs to work on.

STATE OF THE ART COACHING + EQUIPMENT AWARENESS = SUCCESS @ THE ACADEMY

INNOVATION @ THE ACADEMY - INSTANT VIDEO FEEDBACK

The Warren Smith Ski Academy has used video analysis as a coaching tool and means of feedback for many years (all Academy courses have Instant Video Feedback). Visual feedback is one of the best ways to improve skiing skill as it allows skiers to view their performance so they can truly understand what the coach is saying to them.

With the help and investment of Academy Sponsors and Partners, the Warren Smith Ski Academy has developed an innovative way to overcome one of the drawbacks of traditional video analysis - that the analysis does not take place immediately and the skier has to wait until the end of the day before they can watch their performance. This delay can dramatically reduce the impact and effectiveness of the feedback as the skier has forgotten what feelings they experienced and is unable to fully relate to what they are seeing on the screen. Using the latest Sony broadcast digital video technology instant video feedback is possible. The quality of the high definition screens plugged into the cameras allows the Academy's cameraman to be able to immediately replay the skier's run so that feedback can be given on the slopes. Skiers can put the feedback received into practice straight away They can also take home a personalised DVD of their skiing and so have a reference tool that they can study.

Contact:
The Warren Smith Ski Academy
A Snowsport Synergy Ltd company
UK Office: +44 (0)1525 374757
Swiss Office: +41 (0) 79 359 6566
Website: www.warrensmith@skiacademy.com
Email: admin@snowsportsynergy.com
Warren Smith Profile www.soulsports.co.uk/warrensmith

THE WARREN SMITH ACADEMY TEAM

The Warren Smith Ski Academy brings together some of the sports top professionals to create the ultimate coaching team guaranteeing ski technique solutions. Success is achieved by evolving traditional methods of coaching and focusing on the enjoyment and adrenaline factor. Skier Confidence is increased as levels of skill are developed. Awareness of new ski technology is raised at the Academy, showing skiers how to get greater sensations and more from their equipment.

Full profiles of the Academy Team members are available on the Academy website - www.warrensmith-skiacademy.com

GAP YEAR COURSE

The Warren Smith Ski Academy is this year introducing its first GAP year program in association with BASI (www.basi.org.uk). The program will run for nine weeks in the prestigious resort of Verbier and will take students up to BASI 3 ski instructor level.

For more information of the GAP year course send an email to warrensmith@snowsportsynergy.com or call 01525 374757.

IN ASSOCIATION WITH

8 JANUARY - 12 MARCH

Personal Performance Development
BASI Trainee Instructor Course
BASI Central Theme
First Aid Course
Avalanche and Mountain Awareness Course
Ski Maintenance Training
Sport Psychology + Science
Ski Biomechanics in Ski Instruction
Professional Video Filming + Analysis
Pilates and Ski Specific Physical Training
Hands on Ski School Experience

For More info call UK office on +44 (0)1525 374757

Carving Notes

STEEPS NOTES

MOGULS NOTES

FREERIDE NOTES